Native American Tribes: The History and Culture of the Navajo

By Charles River Editors

1891 drawing of a Navajo wearing silver conchos and other jewelry.

About Charles River Editors

Charles River Editors was founded by Harvard and MIT alumni to provide superior editing and original writing services, with the expertise to create digital content for publishers across a vast range of subject matter. In addition to providing original digital content for third party publishers, Charles River Editors republishes civilization's greatest literary works, bringing them to a new generation via ebooks.

Sign up here to receive updates about free books as we publish them, and visit Our Kindle Author Page to browse today's free promotions and our most recently published Kindle titles.

Introduction

A Navajo weaver working next to sheep

The Navajo

From the "Trail of Tears" to Wounded Knee and Little Bighorn, the narrative of American history is incomplete without the inclusion of the Native Americans that lived on the continent before European settlers arrived in the 16th and 17th centuries. Since the first contact between natives and settlers, tribes like the Sioux, Cherokee, and Navajo have both fascinated and perplexed outsiders with their history, language, and culture. In Charles River Editors' Native American Tribes series, readers can get caught up to speed on the history and culture of North America's most famous native tribes in the time it takes to finish a commute, while learning interesting facts long forgotten or never known.

The Navajo are one of the most famous tribes in the United States, even though many of the important events in the people's history have been overlooked with the passage of time. Still one of the biggest Native American groups in America, the Navajo are typically associated with the Southwest and other tribes like the Pueblo, and they are popularly remembered for the Code Talkers of World War II, who used the Navajo language to provide the American military with a code that could not be deciphered by enemy cryptologists.

Unfortunately, the 19th century was full of hardships for the Navajo, particularly as American settlers pushed west in the later stages of the 1800s. They engaged in conflicts with the Americans, but eventually they had to make the Long Walk, a march of over 300 miles from their homes to a reservation. Like the Cherokee's Trail of Tears, the Long Walk was an unmitigated disaster for the Navajo, who only suffered more adversity in the years after the Long Walk as their lands and livelihoods were reduced.

Nevertheless, the Navajo have successfully maintained their culture and traditions, which are some of the oldest and richest in North America, as evidenced by the Code Talkers in the 1940s. As anthropologists and scholars become more refined, they have been able to trace the Navajo's history and identity in ways that allow them to compare and contrast to neighboring Native American groups, which has led to a better understanding of their ancestors as well.

Today, the Navajo people are the second largest federally-recognized tribe of the United States with over 300,000 members, which represents over 15% of the total Native American population in America. *Native American Tribes: The History and Culture of the Navajo* comprehensively covers the culture and history of the famous tribe, profiling their origins, their famous leaders, and their lasting legacy. Along with pictures of important people, places, and events, you will learn about the Navajo like you never have before, in no time at all.

Native American Tribes: The History and Culture of the Navajo
About Charles River Editors
Introduction
   Introductory Note
   Chapter 1: The Navajo Identity
   Chapter 2: Moving to the Southwest
   Chapter 3: Origins of the Navajo
   Chapter 4: The Navajo Lifestyle
   Chapter 5: Contact with Whites
   Chapter 6: The Long Walk
   Chapter 7: The Modern Period
   Chapter 8: The Navajo Today
   Bibliography

Introductory Note

Spelling of proper names of individuals, various Native American groups, and locations can vary due to historical, cultural, and linguistic tradition. While "Navaho" was long considered the proper spelling, "Navajo" is now recognized as accurate. Furthermore, application of the singular Navajo rather than Navajos is used according to scholarly and anthropological criterion despite the fact that several Navajo subgroups and other Native American groups referenced use the plural (as do various non-academic sources). Additionally, while the term "tribe" is widely considered socially insensitive and historically inaccurate, it is applied here in deference to the Navajo Nation, which refers to itself as such.

Chapter 1: The Navajo Identity

The Navajo people are speakers of a Na-Dené Southern Athabaskan language known as *Diné bizaad* (meaning "People speech"). The language comprises two mutually-intelligible dialects closely related to the Apache language, which suggests that both the Navajo and Apache were once been a conjoined group who then migrated from northwestern Canada and/or eastern Alaska, where the majority of Athabaskan speakers are known to have originated. In fact, speakers of various other regional Athabaskan languages of Canada can still understand the Navajo language despite the geographic and linguistic differences that grew between them over time. Similarly, the Navajo of today share a general linguistic pattern with Apachean-related groups like the Jicarilla and Mescalero Apache of New Mexico, with their language differences being primarily a matter of dialect and intra-tribal colloquialisms.

During the first decades of the 17th century, Spanish explorers used the term *Apachu de Nabajo* to collectively refer to the sheep-raising people in the Chama Valley region east of the San Juan River and northwest of present-day Santa Fe, New Mexico. By the 1640s, they began applying the term "Navajo", a modified Tewa Puebloan word, to the Diné, who at that time referred to themselves as the *Nadené* ("The People").

Although the Navajo generally refer to themselves as Navajo" today, the term *Nadené* is still often used among members of the group. In 1994, it was proposed that the official designation be changed from "Navajo" to "Diné", but it was rejected by the Navajo Nation council because Diné represented the time of suffering before the Long Walk. As a result, Navajo remains the appropriate designation.

Chapter 2: Moving to the Southwest

Archaeological evidence indicates that the first significant settlement of the Southwest's "Four-Corners" region was built by three major "Puebloan" cultural groups: the Anasazi (a term given to them by the Navajo and otherwise known as the "Pueblo Peoples"), the Mogollon (the so-called "Gila Wilderness People"), and the Hohokam. The Patayan and Sinagua also played significant roles, but scholars are still unsure about the extent and timing of their participation in the region.

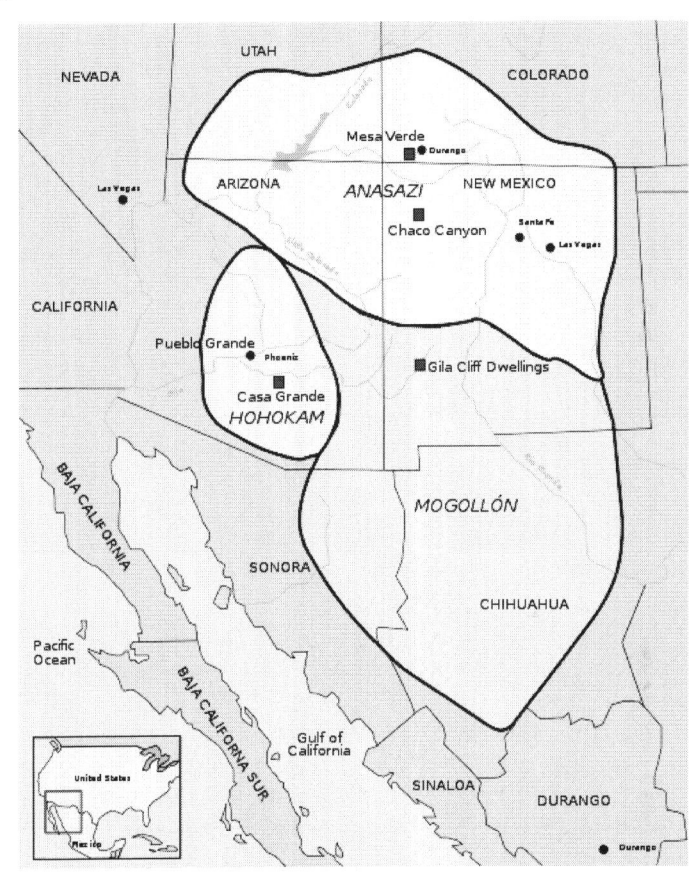

The Anasazi are believed to have settled the area north and west of the Colorado River before reaching their peak around 1050-1150 A.D., but they abandoned most of their settlements by 1200. The Mogollon are thought to have occupied a larger swath of land south of the Anasazi in what is today New Mexico, western Texas, and the northern Mexico states of Sonora and Chihuahua, reaching their peak around 1000. However, like the Anasazi, they also moved out of the region within two centuries. The comparatively smaller Hohokam culture settled in southern Arizona around 700 and disappeared just 500 years later. While it is generally accepted that these groups migrated southeast towards the Rio Grande Valley and regrouped there, there is no consensus as to why they abandoned their former settlements. One well-supported theory, however, cites the arrival of the Navajo, Apache, and what remained of the Ute to the Southwest.

Exactly *when* that happened remains a point of scholarly contention.

One common hypothesis dates the arrival of the Navajo, Apache, and Ute to what is referred to as the "Dinétah" archaeological phase of the Upper San Juan River drainage area in northwestern New Mexico, southwestern Colorado, southeastern Utah, and northeastern Arizona. This would place the Navajo's arrival around 1500. Another common contention is that these groups first entered the U. S. Southwest during the Historic period after the Puebloan Revolt of 1680, during which the indigenous Pueblo nations of the Southwest expelled Spanish colonizers and restored self-rule. According to Barry Pritzker in *Native American Encyclopedia: History, Culture, and Peoples*, archaeological and historical evidence suggests that the Athabaskan ancestors of the Navajo and Apache entered the Southwest around 1400 CE, but most archaeologists dispute this date now. In any case, historians regard the Navajo and Apache as relative new arrivals, first entering the Southwest as hunter-gatherers and establishing villages north and between territories inhabited by the Anasazi, Mogollon, and Hohokam. The Ute, meanwhile, established themselves in the Great Basin.

Scholars today generally agree that the Navajo and Apache peoples were once one undifferentiated group of hunter-gatherers living amongst a larger collection of Athapascan-speaking people from Canada and possibly Alaska. Some have even theorized that the Navajo and Apache once constituted a subgroup of the Ute people.

Eventually separating from the linguistic conglomerate to which they previously belonged, the Navajo-Apache migrated south along the high Plains of the United States, following the edge of the Rocky Mountains. Encountering the comparatively more aggressive Plains groups along the way (who at this time lived in fortified villages and carried on small-scale farming), the Navajo learned basic farming techniques applicable to raising corn and squash, as well as the art of crafting pottery, which the Plains groups are thought to have learned from the Eastern Woodland groups. After coming into contact with the Puebloan groups of the Southwest (the Anasazi, Mogollon, Hohokam and proto-Hopi), they further expanded their knowledge of farming and adopted an even more sedentary lifestyle. Meanwhile, the Apache remained more mobile.

After some experimentation with settling pueblo-like villages and building *hogans,* permanent wooden and stone structures, the Navajo and Apache began raiding Puebloan settlements, which presumably set off their historic mass exodus. Though they were less aggressive than the Plains tribes, the Navajo and Apache were both fundamentally more aggressive than the Puebloan peoples of the time, and they essentially divided the Southwest between themselves after pushing the Pueblo out.

A NAVAJO HOUSE

Although they ultimately developed two separate cultures, the Navajo and Apache would subsequently unite against the Spanish from the 16th century all the way until the early 19th century. They would also fight together against the Mexicans from 1821-1848 and then the U.S. government after the Mexican-American War.

Chapter 3: Origins of the Navajo

To a greater degree than many other Native American groups, the sociocultural and geographic evolution of the Navajo people is readily reflected in their mythology and religious structure. While some myths relate the emergence of the first people and describe various locations beneath the surface of the Earth, others serve to explain the origin of various rites and rituals the Navajo have performed through the centuries.

Creation of the First Man and First Woman

Late one autumn, the distant sound of a great voice was heard calling from the east. A moment later, four mysterious beings appeared. These were White Body (the god of this world), Blue Body (the "Sprinkler"), Yellow Body, and Black Body (the god of fire). Using signs but not words, the four tried to instruct the creatures of Earth which had gathered before them as to their purpose, but their message was not understood. For three days in succession, the four appeared again, each time using signs and each time not being understood. Finally, on the fourth day, Black Body spoke to the creatures in their own language, saying, "You do not seem to understand our signs so I must tell you what they mean. We want to make people who look more like us. You have bodies like us but you have the teeth, the feet, and the claws of beasts and insects. The new humans will have hands and feet like us. Also, you are unclean and smell bad. Be clean when we return."

On the 12th day, as the creatures bathed themselves — the females drying their skin with yellow cornmeal and the men using white cornmeal — they heard the sounds of the approaching gods. When they arrived, Blue Body and Black Body each carried a sacred buckskin, White Body carried two ears of corn (one yellow and one white), and Yellow Body carried two eagle feathers. Laying one buckskin on the ground with the head pointed to the west, White Body placed the two ears of corn upon it with their tips pointed to the east, while Yellow Body placed a white eagle feather beneath the white ear and a yellow eagle feather beneath the yellow ear. The ears were then covered with the second buckskin, with its head pointed to the east.

The gods then told the creatures to stand back and allow the sacred wind to enter. From the east, the white wind blew between the skins, and from the west the yellow wind blew. While the wind was blowing, eight gods known as the "Mirage People" arrived and circled the skins four times. As they did, the eagle feathers, which protruded from beneath the skins, could be seen moving. When the Mirage People completed their walk, the top skin was removed, revealing a man and woman lying there in place of the ears. The white ear became the first man, and the yellow ear became the first woman. The gods instructed man and woman to live together as husband and wife, giving birth to the Native American race.

Legend of the Night Chant

In most Native American societies, medicine men and shamans are believed to have the ability to prevent disease through ceremony and ritual. Termed "ritualistic prayers" in the Navajo tradition, the *Kieje Hatal* (Night Chant) is considered one of the most important chants and is rooted in this mythological legend.

A long time ago, three brothers lived among their people, known as the *Diné*. The oldest brother was rich, the middle was a roving gambler, and the youngest was still a growing boy. Their only sister lived with her husband a short distance away.

The middle brother frequently took property belonging to his brothers and would then travel to distant corners of the earth to gamble. Upon his return, he would always tell of the wonders he had seen and of the secrets revealed to him by the "Holy People" he encountered. Always doubting his honesty, his brothers called him *Bith Ahatini*, "The Dreamer."

One day the eldest and youngest brothers wished to go hunting without *Bith Ahatini,* so they secretly invited their brother-in-law to come along. After four days, "The Dreamer" realized he had been purposely left out, so he set out in search of his brothers, hoping to catch up with them and help carry their game and be rewarded with a pelt or two for his efforts. By nightfall, *Bith Ahatini* had not yet found his brothers, but as he stood near a deep canyon he heard voices from the depths. Peering over the edge he saw countless crows flying back and forth from one side to the other, passing in and out of holes in the walls. Then he heard a human voice call, "They say! They say! They say!"

"Yes, yes! What's the matter now?" came a response.

"Two people were killed today," the voice said.

"Who were they? Who were they?"

"Ana-hail-ihi, killed at sunrise, and Igak-izhi, killed at dusk, by the People of the Earth," the first voice said. "They went in search of meat and hunters shot arrows into them. We are sorry but they did not heed our warning. It is too late to help them now so let us go on with the chant." Though frightened, *Bith Ahatini* stayed to listen and watch.

From the deep recesses of the canyon came a muffled song: "The gods are singing!", *Bith Ahatini* thought. And from within the openings he saw the glow of a fire, with many dancers moving in unison as they kept time with rattles. Throughout the night, he watched as light from the fire flickered from wall to wall and singing and dancing continued. At daylight the dancing stopped, so "The Dreamer" resumed his search for his brothers.

After a short time, *Bith Ahatini* came upon his brothers, resting with their heavy packs of game.

"Here comes 'The Dreamer,'" said his older brother. "I will wager that he has something marvelous to tell us!"

"You must have slept near here last night," his brother-in-law said, "for you are too far from home to have traveled this distance since daylight."

"I slept near a canyon that is surely holy," replied *Bith Ahatini*. "Many people had gathered to dance, the gods sang, and--"

"--There! I told you he would have some lie to tell!" interrupted the oldest brother, picking up his pack and moving on.

"No - go ahead!" urged his brother-in-law. "Tell me the rest of the story!"

The younger brother, also not believing, took up his pack to catch up with his brother.

Addressing his brother-in-law, "The Dreamer" related what he had seen and heard, saying, "Surely, you or my brothers must have killed the people they spoke about."

"Oh, no! It was none of us!" his brother-in-law assured him. "We have killed no people. Yesterday one of us shot a crow and last night a magpie, but there was no harm done!"

"I fear there was," said *Bith Ahatini*. "They are hunters like you, disguised as birds, in search of meat for the Holy People!"

"The Dreamer" and his brother-in-law then hurried to catch up with the others.

As they followed the path, his brother-in-law suddenly burst, "Look! Here come four mountain sheep. Hurry! We can head them off!" Following the sheep, the brothers were led into the canyon where *Bith Ahatini* had heard the voices and witnessed the dance. As the three hunters dropped back, "The Dreamer" ran ahead and hid himself near the top of the trail. As the sheep approached, he drew his bow and aimed, but his fingers would not release the arrow, allowing them to pass unharmed. Three more times he attempted to kill the sheep but could not.

As he fell to the ground cursing himself and the sheep, he watched as the four sheep transformed themselves into gods, all wearing masks.

"From where did you come?" *Bith Ahatini* asked.

"Kinni-nikai," one replied.

"Where are you going?"

"To Taegyil to hold another ceremony four days from now. Would you like to come along?"

"I could not travel that distance in just four days."

Persuaded to make the journey, he was told to disrobe, after which one of the gods breathed upon him, and suddenly he was wearing the same clothing as the four gods. Taking four steps eastward, they all changed into sheep and bounded away along the canyon's rim.

Now worried that *Bith Ahatini* had not returned, the brothers ventured to the trail where he had last been seen. Following his tracks, the eldest brother soon found his brother's clothes--his bow and arrows lying neatly upon them—and noticed many sets of footprints. The eldest brother found that the footprints merged into the trail of five mountain sheep. He now realized he had been wrong about the "The Dreamer."

As sheep, *Bith Ahatini* and the gods traveled for four days, coming upon a large *hogan* inside which were many Holy People, both gods and human. Inside, he saw four large jewel posts upon which hung the gods' masks. The eastern post was of white shell, the southern of turquoise, the western of abalone, and the northern of jet. Two jeweled pipes lay near a god, who filled both with tobacco, lit them, and then passed one to his right and one to his left. Everyone in the hogan smoked, and the last to receive the pipes were two large owls sitting on each side of the eastern entrance.

As the ceremony began, some of the gods had beautiful paintings on white deerskins, which resembling those the Navajo make with colored sands. The gods spread the art on the floor. *Bith Ahatini* paid careful attention to all the songs, prayers, and dance movements, and by the time the chant ended, he had learned every details of the *Kieje Hatal*, the "Night Chant."

Permitted to return to his people long enough to perform the "chant" for his younger brother and to conduct it for the people of his village afflicted with illness or wickedness, "The Dreamer" then returned to the gods at Taegyil, where he now lives. Carried on by his younger brother, the ceremony is today known as *Kieje Hatal* ("Night Chant") or *Yebichai Hatal* ("The Chant of Paternal Gods.")

Myth and Practical Rites

For the Navajo culture, there is a direct relationship between many of their myths and the rituals and ceremonies. Myths essentially establish historic precedence. Similarly, a number of practical "specialist" jobs within the Navajo religious system, for which the individual is paid according to his reputation and length of ceremony, are also rooted in myth. Most prestigious, perhaps, is the role of *diagnostician*, an individual skilled in various forms of divination aimed at determining which ritual or remedy is appropriate to counteract a given ailment. Since the Navajo believe that most physical and mental illnesses are supernatural in origin, a *diagnostician* may prescribe purification by sweating or induced vomiting, herbal remedies, conducting song and prayer intended to rid the body of negative energies, fend off psychic attack, or appease malevolent spirits.

While various forms of ritual and ceremony are associated with most Native American groups of both the past and present, no group is more closely associated with "craft" than the Navajo. Of course, it is also one of the least understood aspects of the Navajo culture. Although the Navajo are believed to share common spiritual concepts and beliefs with other indigenous groups of North America, their spiritual belief system is shrouded in mystery yet spotlighted by popular folklore. Since nearly half of all known Navajo myths depict witches or the practice of witchcraft, anthropologists assume it is very much a part of the Navajo psyche.

A topic of ethnographic research for several renowned cultural anthropologists like Clyde Kluckhohn, who lived among both the Navajo and Hopi in the early to mid-20th century, it has been speculated that while nature-based religious practices date back millennia in the Athabaskan-speaking culture, it was most likely Hopi/Puebloan influence that spurred the Navajo's interest in ritual and, specifically, the practice of witchcraft. As Kluckhohn explained in works published in the 1940s, when the Hopi lived among the Navajo during the 18th century to escape drought and famine in their own lands, they not only taught the Navajo practical Puebloan arts like the making of pottery and advanced farming methods but also shared their mystical arts, involving the practice of witchcraft as well. From that time on, the Navajo and Hopi continued to exchange goods and technologies, with the Navajo trading rugs and silver to the Hopi for ceremonial items, and they would come together yearly to practice magic. Even as recently as 1946, the Navajo continued to borrow ritual methodology and beliefs from the Hopi, deeming them, "skillful black magicians."[1] According to the Navajo, the Hopi believe that death is always due to witchcraft, a revelation believed to have spurred the Navajo to practice witchcraft and counter-witchcraft.

Although it is difficult to separate popular "hype" from authentic practices, the realm of Navajo "craft" appears to have several distinctive elements. For example, *'Ańt'įįzhį* is thought to be the most common form of witchcraft, with practitioners (who are most often male) called *'ánt'įįhnii,* meaning "witch people." *'Ánt'įįhnii* traditionally learn their craft from a parent or grandparent, though sometimes also from a spouse. Initiation into *'Ańt'įįzhį* is said to involve the taking of life, typically that of a close relative or sibling, but other than oral accounts, there is

---

[1] Kluckhohn, Clyde. Navaho Witchcraft. Page 23.

no evidence of this activity. Other practices commonly associated with *'Ańt'įįzhį* are necrophilia, grave-robbing, and incest.   HYPE - IGNORANCE

By and large, Navajo witchcraft is said to center around the administering of powdered corpses known as *'áńt'į* or "corpse poison," manifesting as various symptoms including fainting, swelling of the tongue, lockjaw or even death. Popular lore describes Navajo witches as gathering in caves or other secluded spots where they assume animal form to perform countermagic.

Due to popular lore and depictions in various movies and literature, *yee naaldlooshii*, or "Skinwalkers" is the aspect of magic most closely related to Navajo witchcraft. *'Ánt'įihnii* (shape-shifting witches who become "Skinwalkers") are said to use animal forms to covertly travel and perform various secret rituals and cast spells. This, of course, is based on popular lore, with no basis in science. Shape-shifting is, however, a common motif within many Native American religious systems.

Chapter 4: The Navajo Lifestyle

The designation "Navajo" comes from the late 17th century via Spanish explorers who derived the name from the Tewa *navahū*, meaning "fields adjoining a ravine." Like other Apachean groups like the Apache and Ute, the Navajo were traditionally semi-nomadic from the 16th-20th centuries, but their extended kinship groups had seasonal dwellings to accommodate livestock, agriculture, and serve as gathering places for ritual. It also seems quite likely that trading and raiding, which saw their parties travel great distances, were also part of their traditional economy for considerable periods of time.

Historically, Navajo society is fundamentally a matrilineal system in which women owned the livestock and land, and people traced their descent through the mother and organized primarily along the lines of kinship. By tradition, daughters or other female relatives were in line to receive the generational property inheritance, which may be meager but could also include one or more houses, property, farmland, livestock, and other valued items. This has changed in modern times due to assimilation and U.S. laws; Navajo children often inherit from both parents today.

A picture of a Navajo woman and child, circa 1880-1910

Once married, Navajo men typically moved in with their bride and lived among her mother's family and clan, with the mother's brothers assuming responsibility for the upbringing, marriage, and general guidance of their sister's children. By tradition, it is said that children are "born to" the mother's clan and "born for" the father's clan. With this distinction, fathers were not permitted to discipline their own children because technically they were of a different clan.

As the marriage arrangement indicates, clan membership is central to Navajo social organization. It is a complex *exogamous* kinship system through which a Navajo belongs to his mother's clan but also considers himself or herself related to the clansmen of his or her father. As with most matrilineal societies around the world, no Navajo may take a mate who belongs to the clan of either parent, and more traditional Navajo families extend this stipulation to clans even socially associated with either parent. Invariably, a Navajo had particular categorical obligations to relatives on both the mother's and father's sides of the family, as well as to relatives by marriage (with relatives obligated to similar reciprocal duties and courtesies). In some settings, non-biologically related clan members could claim family-member status and even assert rights over a deceased's property.

Given this system, perhaps it's no surprise that the Navajo code of ethics towards all is "Behave towards everyone as you behave with your relatives."[2]

By tradition, the *hogan* (the standard Navajo home) is built to either accommodate a man or a woman. While both models are made of wood and covered in mud, with the door facing east to welcome the sun, male hogans are square or conical with a distinct rectangular entrance, while a female hogan is eight-sided. The Navajo also construct several other types of *hogans* for lodging and ceremonial use, such as for the *kinaaldá* ceremony. Though they were commonly made in the traditional manner well into the 20th century, today they are regarded primarily as places of ceremony. Even so, while many modern Navajo live in apartments or standard houses, many prefer the solidly-constructed, log-walled *hogan* to any other option when practical. The spiritual song "*Hozhooji*" ("The Blessingway") describes the first *hogan* as being built by Coyote, with instruction from the Beaver People, for First Man, First Woman, and Talking God.

A Navajo *Hogan*

---

[2] *Navajo People—the Diné website.*

According to Navajo oral tradition, during the 1850s, a Navajo man named Atsidi Sani who had been befriended by a Mexican ironsmith took the first step towards establishing the Navajo people as premier silversmiths. Having first learned to forge iron bridles, he then turned his attention and natural artistic abilities to crafting silver, and he subsequently taught his four sons this new craft.

Becoming known for converting U. S. quarters into silver bells, Atsidi Sani's sons taught other Navajo the craft, and decorative bells became a common item sewn onto Navajo leggings and sashes. Silversmiths soon produced silver headstalls for their horses, as well as silver bow guards, tobacco cases, necklaces, buttons, and *conchas* (silver disks mounted on belts). Around 1880, the next significant phase in Navajo art began when a Navajo silversmith mounted a turquoise stone on a silver object. Virtually overnight, this combination proved highly appealing, prompting the formation of a Navajo craftsmen class. The tools and techniques were quickly attained by many, and traders now kept pliers, hammers, files, sandpaper, and crucibles in stock.

By 1890, however, the U. S. Government sought to marginalize Navajo smithies first by enforcing existing laws prohibiting the defacement of U. S. coins, which were considered "government property". This forced smiths to rely on traders for raw materials, like Herman Schweizer, a German immigrant who became one of the largest collectors of American Indian art in the world. Schweizer paid Navajo and other Native American craftsmen to make light-weight, cheaply-made silver handicrafts for a fraction of what they were worth. While this helped establish Navajo silversmith artistry, by World War I factories were stamping out copies of hand-crafted jewelry with no compensation to Navajo artisans since the Navajo could not patent nor copyright their methods and designs.

Although Navajo art and craft production mostly provided only a supplementary source of income, the Navajo have come increasingly identified with their finely-crafted turquoise and silver jewelry, as well as indigenous sand painting, feather work, and pottery. A 2004 study by the Navajo Division of Economic Development found that at least 60% of all Navajo families have at least one member producing arts and crafts.

The so-called "squash blossom" necklace, the Navajo's signature piece of jewelry, first appeared in the 1880s. Thought to have derived from popular Spanish-Mexican pomegranate designs, Navajo silversmiths adopted the "naja" (*najahe* in Navajo) symbol for the silver crescent pendant traditionally suspended from the "squash blossom" necklace.

A Navajo squash blossom necklace

While the Navajo are thought to have come into the Southwest with their own weaving traditions, oral history describes them as learning to weave cotton on upright looms from Pueblo peoples (perhaps the Hopi). The first Spaniards to visit the region frequently spoke about "Navajo blankets." By the 18th century, the Navajo had begun to trade for Bayeta red yarn, a red wool that acquires its red color from carminic acid derived from the Mesoamerican cochineal beetle. This color complemented local black, grey, and white wool, as well as wool dyed with indigo.

Utilizing the Puebloan upright loom, the Navajo produced extremely fine utilitarian blankets prized by Ute and Plains indigenous groups, as well as European settlers. These aptly-named "Chiefs' Blankets", blankets only chiefs or the very wealthy could afford, were characterized by horizontal stripes and minimal patterning in red, though the design evolved over time.

The completion of the railway system around 1830 accommodated the importation of cheap blankets, so Navajo weavers shifted their focus from blankets to rugs for the increasingly non-Native clientele. The rail service did, however, allow commercially-dyed wool from Philadelphia to be shipped west, which greatly expanded the Navajo weaver's color palettes and made their products even more attractive for market. As European pioneers moved west and set up trading posts near Native American settlements, many arranged to buy Navajo rugs by the pound, which they sent back east to be sold by the bale. Traders often encouraged local indigenous groups to weave blankets and rugs with distinctive non-traditional styles to make them more commercially viable. Consequently, a number of competing styles evolved, including the "Two Gray Hills" (predominantly black and white with traditional patterns), *Teec Nos Pos* (colorful with a very complex pattern), "Crystal" (created by weaver J. B. Moore), "Klagetoh" (diamond-shape patterns), and "Red Mesa" (bold diamond patterns).

Chapter 5: Contact with Whites

The oldest known recorded account of a Navajo encounter with Europeans occurred in 1629, when Franciscan Friar Alonso de Benevides acted as intermediary between the Spanish and Navajo to negotiate peaceful relations. Technically speaking, this "Navajo" group should be considered the progenitors of modern Navajo, or *proto*-Navajo. As the Europeans settled along the Rio Grande Valley, at some point the European supply of horses and sheep became too tempting for Navajo raiders, who found it more economically advantageous to raid Spanish settlements than rely on their own crops or wild game. Thus, when De Benevides wrote of the Navajo custom of raising sheep, he was referring to an issue of potential conflict that his entire mission was attempting to avert. Ultimately, the availability of Spanish livestock led to the first of many confrontations with white settlers who established ranches on Navajo land, and by the late 17th century, the Spanish began sending military expeditions against the Navajo in the Mount Taylor and Chuska Mountain regions of New Mexico; actions they justified by terming the Navajo "warring."

However, historians do not believe "warring" is a fair designation. Though recognized as raiders and plunderers throughout early history, even by modern Navajo, most scholars contend that the Navajo people could never justifiably be designated a "warring" group because regardless of how seemingly organized and aggressive they may have been, they lacked the fundamental political unity required for military organization. They had no tribal "chiefs" in the traditional sense, they were divided into many bands (as were the Apache and Ute), and Navajo raids were sporadic and opportunistic expeditions and conducted by small, independent parties. While some of the men conducted raids, the bulk of the Navajo people remained semi-sedentary, farming, raising livestock, and crafting. Historians also note that if the Navajo had sought to dominate the Southwest through subjugation, they could have united with the more hostile Apache and easily established regional dominance. Instead, they maintained friendly relations with Puebloan groups for several centuries.

This reality is further emphasized by the fact that the Navajo not only raided European settlements but also conducted raids on various Native American pueblos in New Mexico and Mexico proper as well. This also led to frequent retaliation by the Mexicans, who often took them captive. Additionally, while the Navajo sphere extended further west than any other indigenous group of the region, they initially restricted themselves to northern New Mexico, which is why they took such offence to white settlers coming upon their land.

By the 1720s, all tribes neighboring "Navajoland" had acquired firearms and munitions from English and French traders, and the Plains tribes had completely redeveloped their cultures around the horse. Once the Comanche, Pawnee, and Wichita had both guns and horses, the Navajo, who did not establish such trade arrangements, fell to disadvantage. With the social and economic benefits of raiding now fading and becoming increasingly more dangerous, the Navajo began to rely much more heavily on an economy consisting of hunting, sheep-raising, and farming-gathering, a multi-level economic system no other Athapascan subgroup adopted. Still, when opportunities arose to acquire additional food, livestock, or arms, the Navajo did not hesitate.

However, the introduction of sheep-raising to Navajo economy soon created a new social dynamic. Sheep-raising, farming and gathering became the exclusive domain of women, and hunting and raiding were done exclusively by men, which resulted in Navajo women suddenly acquiring unprecedented power. As Navajo men asserted their rights to bring home Spanish and Puebloan women as concubines, Navajo women countered by expanding their control over inheritance and property. By the mid-18th century, Navajo men were devoting more time to developing religious practices. While the curing of the sick (both physically and mentally) remained the primary purpose of religion, men began ritualizing their relationship with the supernatural world, introducing many new chants, songs, and dances.

During the latter half of the 18th century, the state of "Indian affairs" of the Southwest took a significant turn when Spanish Colonial Governor Juan Bautista de Anza established alliances with the primary Plains groups and may have even armed them. This arrangement coerced the Ute into cooperating with the Spanish, who used the Ute and Comanche to intimidate the Navajo Nation into a quasi-alliance with Spain. With the Apache conducting search-and-destroy missions on behalf of the Spanish, the Navajo found themselves hemmed in by Spanish domination. Persuading the Navajo to sign various peace pacts, Spanish authorities frequently faulted Navajo leaders for apparent treaty violations, mistakenly assuming that a band leader spoke for the entire Navajo population. Since raiding constituted the only basis for organization, leaders who did not routinely lead raiding parties had virtually no authority, and those who did only had authority on raids. As a result of misunderstandings, relations between the Spanish and Navajo remained in a constant state of flux.

A portrait of de Anza

By 1821, colonial authorities of "New Spain", the Spanish designation for Southwestern U. S. and parts of northern Mexico, decided to establish political independence in the form of a new nation called "Mexico." However, Napoleon's assaults on the Spanish Army back in Europe during the early 19th century greatly shook and undermined Spanish colonial resolve, which worked to the Navajo's benefit. By the time Mexico achieved its political independence in 1821, the Navajo were virtually autonomous again. Although this would soon degenerate into decades of retaliatory raiding between the Navajo and Mexican people, with a booming slave trade developing on both sides, the opening of the Santa Fe Trail that same year provided access to a whole new selection of trade goods, and white traders established direct relationships with many Navajo families.

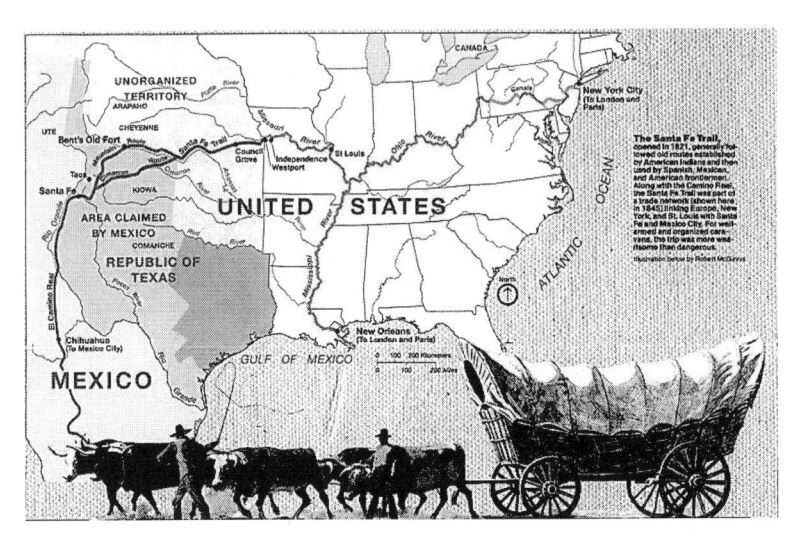

The route of the Santa Fe Trail

Chapter 6: The Long Walk

Unfortunately for the Navajo, the level of autonomy they had as a result of Mexico's independence gave way after the United States claimed lands conquered during the Mexican-American War. Circumstances reached a new critical point in 1846 when Colonel Stephen W. Kearny took possession of "Navajoland" on behalf of the United States during that war, which lasted from 1846-1848.

By 1849, relations between the Navajo, Spanish, and Hopi were at the breaking point. Then came a division of land implemented by the U. S. government, which cut their range in half. The Bonneville Treaty of 1858 further reduced Navajo landholdings and exacerbated the situation even more.

The Civil War disrupted the frontier, beginning in 1861. The withdrawal of federal troops from the Southwest left settlers vulnerable to raids by the Navajo and Apache. In 1862, General James H. Carleton, who had assumed command of the military forces in New Mexico, formulated a plan to subdue the Navajo permanently by relocating them to a reservation at the Bosque Redondo in New Mexico near Fort Sumner. This would essentially make the Navajo prisoners of war. By the spring of 1863, 400 Mescalero were under guard at Bosque Redondo, and by the close of that year about 200 Navajo had been corralled there as well.

Carleton

Early in 1864, General Carleton enlisted the aid of famed frontiersman Kit Carson, charging him with telling the Navajo, "You have deceived us too often, and robbed and murdered our people too long, to trust you again at large in your own country. This war shall be pursued against you if it takes years, now that we have begun, until you cease to exist or move. There can be no other talk on the subject."[3]

As a result, U. S. Army troops under Carson invaded the Navajo stronghold at Cañon de Chelly and burned Navajo farms and homes, killing 23, capturing 34, and forcing 200 to surrender. By year's end, some 8,000 Navajo had been forced at gunpoint to walk more than 300 miles from their traditional lands in eastern Arizona and western New Mexico to Bosque Redondo. The journey is now known as the "Long Walk of the Navajo."

---

[3] *Sides, Hampton.* Blood and Thunder. *Page 344.*

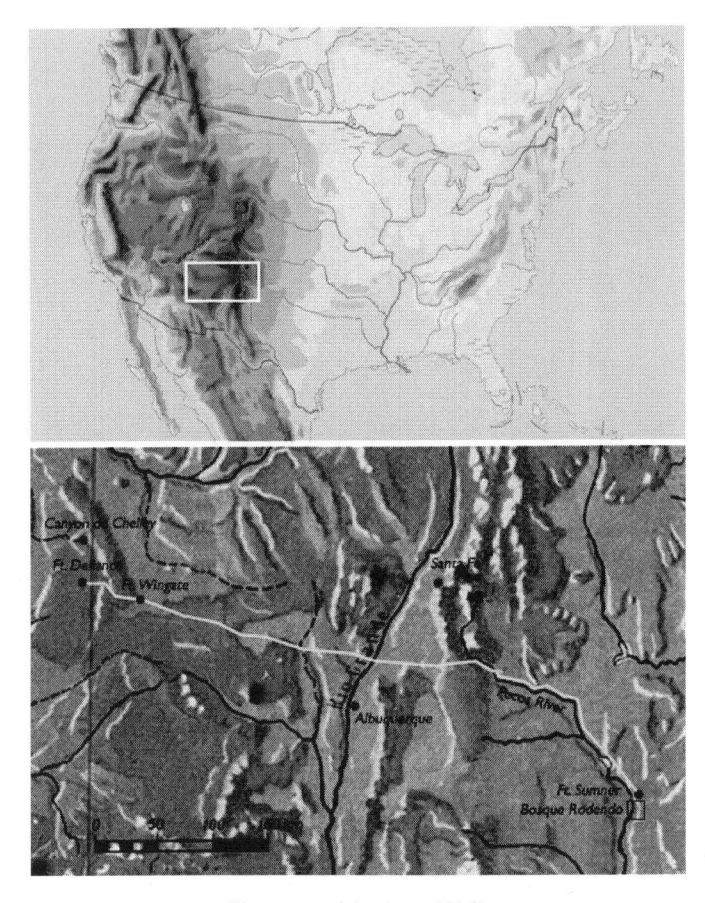

The route of the Long Walk

Anthropologist Thomas Csordas once wrote that the "collective trauma of the Long Walk...is critical to contemporary Navajos' sense of identity as a people." During the Long Walk, thousands died or fell to disease soon after arriving at the camp. In all, some 53 different forced marches occurred between 1864 and the end of 1866. By the spring of 1865, more than 9,000 Navajo and members of a number of other indigenous groups swept up in Army raids were forcibly settled on an area of just 40 square miles, all under military guard.

A picture of Navajo during the Long Walk

Bosque Redondo, Spanish for "round forest", was fraught with problems. A costly endeavor for the U. S. Government from its inception, water and firewood were major issues from the start; the water was brackish and the "round forest" was quite small.

On top of that, the biggest issue facing the Navajo people regarded their day-to-day safety. The 400 Mescalero Apaches who had been placed there before their arrived had already established their dominance, and with a long tradition of raiding each other's camps, the two groups were constantly at odds during their encampment. Furthermore, Bosque Redondo was intended to accommodate 5,000 people at most, not the 10,000 men, women, and children ultimately packed into it. Within a year, it became apparent that attempts to raise corn were futile. There were constant infestations of army worms, and the flooding of the Pecos River repeatedly washed out the head gates of the irrigation system. Many Navajo began to flee this confinement by the end of 1865, and by 1867 the remaining Navajo refused to plant crops.

Recognizing the endeavor as a colossal failure, in 1868 the reservation was abandoned, and the Navajo were sent home with a new treaty. Of course, that would require another Long Walk. Among the many provisions the Bosque Redondo Treaty of 1868 established were the formal founding of a proper Native American reservation in the Southwest region, restrictions on raiding, a resident Indian Agent and agency, compulsory education for Native American children (the Navajo agreed to send their children to school for a period of 10 years, and the U. S. government agreed to establish schools with one teacher for every 30 Navajo children), the supply of seeds, agricultural implements and other provisions, the right for the Navajo to be protected (by military force if necessary), the establishment of railroads and forts, unspecified compensation to tribal members, and arrangements for the safe return of the Navajo Nation to the reservation established under this treaty.

This memorial commemorates the spot where the new treaty with the Navajo was made in 1868.

On June 18, 1868, the once-scattered *Diné* people set off together on the "Long Walk Home", ultimately returning to their homeland. As one elderly Navajo said of the whole ordeal, ""As I have said, our ancestors were taken captive and driven to Hwéeldi for no reason at all. They were harmless people, and, even to date, we are the same, holding no harm for anybody...Many Navajos who know our history and the story of Hwéeldi say the same."

Chapter 7: The Modern Period

The Navajo and the Hopi

Following the "Long Walk Home" from their imprisonment in Bosque Redondo, the "Navajo Indian Reservation" was established according to the Treaty of 1868. The borders were demarcated as the 37th parallel in the north, the southern border was a line running through Fort Defiance (Apache County, Arizona), the eastern border was a line running through Fort Lyon (Bent County, Colorado), and the western border was at longitude 109°30′. Although the treaty provided for 3.5 million acres of land in the New Mexico Territory inside their four sacred mountains, *Dook'o'oosłííd*, *Dibé Ntsaa*, *Sisnaajini*, and *Tsoodził*, slightly more than half was initially made available. But due to the fact that there were no physical boundaries or signposts to delineate Navajo from Hopi or white lands, many Navajo simply returned to their pre-interment location and ignored formal boundaries. On October 28, 1878, the first formal expansion of the territory occurred when President Rutherford Hayes called for the western boundary to be pushed 20 miles. Further additions were added throughout the late 19th and early 20th century, largely at the expense of neighboring Hopi land.

Though precarious in nature, the relationship between the Navajo and Hopi, the primary Puebloan group that the early Navajo encountered upon reaching the Southwest, is highly significant to Navajo history and their place in modern American society. While the prehistory of the Navajo people is not nearly as well-understood as that of the Hopi, both oral tradition and written history suggest the Navajo and Hopi have lived in close proximity in northeastern Arizona for upwards of 700 years.

According to Hopi oral tradition, during the 1700s several Hopi bands lived among the Navajo to escape drought and famine in their own lands. From that time forward until the mid-19th century, the Navajo and Hopi maintained "guest-friend" relationships, visiting each others' settlements to trade goods and technology. Since the 19th century, however, these two cultures have been at odds over land use and resource access involving a large area of land they mutually share. They reached a complementary arrangement in which the Hopi remained concentrated in large villages while the Navajo moved about freely while grazing their livestock, but the ever-increasing territory claimed by the Navajo led to the first major dispute between these two cultural groups.

By 1820, the land appropriated by the Navajo Nation completely encompassed the Hopi villages at Black Mesa near Kayenta, Arizona. Following their return from forced internment at Bosque Redondo in southeastern New Mexico in 1868, the Navajo initially occupied the reservation set aside for them along the Arizona/New Mexico border, but soon spread—further infringing upon lands the Hopi held sacred. Left with no recourse, the Hopi petitioned the U.S. Government to stop the Navajo from further encroachment.

In 1882, the United States Government granted a 2.5 million-acre tract of land to the Hopi. By this time, however, hundreds of Navajo families had established roots in the area and not only refused to move but continued to expand their borders. Eventually the Navajo Nation grew well inside the 1882 boundaries, forcing the Hopi to repeatedly file letters of protest with the U. S. Department of the Interior. Despite their attempts, the Hopi received no remedy.

At the turn of the 20th century, the United States Government initiated a number of Federal programs designed to neutralize tensions between Native American populations of the Southwest, including the requirement for each "tribe" to set up its own Indian-police and Tribal courts system, as well as appoint a spokesman, nominally a "chief" or some other tribal leader. This added a new dimension to Navajo society, which had never organized under a single leader before.

In 1923, after the discovery of oil on the Navajo-Hopi Reservation, a Navajo tribal government was established to formally address American oil companies asking to lease Navajo land for exploration. In 1934, the Bureau of Indian Affairs (BIA) divided the 2.5 million acres granted the Hopi in 1882 into 18 land-management districts, with only one district (District 6, a boundary around the Hopi villages on the First, Second, and Third Mesas) designated solely for Hopi use. The remaining districts were then deemed the Navajo-Hopi Joint Use Area (JUA), which only exacerbated the ongoing problem as both groups claimed rights not only to its use but its resources.

In 1958, the Hopi Nation filed suit yet again against the Navajo Nation over title to the 1882 reservation lands, with the Secretary of the Interior subsequently granting the Navajo Nation a 50% interest in the remaining Hopi Reservation lands. Between 1961 and 1964, the Hopi Tribal Council signed a number of leases with the U. S. government permitting the drilling for oil and gas and the mining of minerals within Hopi country, again rekindling disputes between the Hopi and Navajo nations over land use and ownership. The conflict further intensified when coal deposits were discovered in the joint-use area and there were reports that the Hopi had already profited to the tune of millions of dollars.

In 1966, BIA Commissioner Robert Bennett issued an administrative order freezing all development and construction in the disputed Hopi-Navajo join-use area, leading to the "Navajo-Hopi Land Settlement/Relocation Act of 1974." The Relocation Act divided the Navajo-Hopi Joint Use Area (JUA) into separate Hopi Partitioned Lands (HPL) and Navajo Partitioned Lands (NPL). As a result, 10,000 Navajo were relocated compared to about 100 Hopi, with many Navajo families ultimately refusing to leave the area known as Big Mountain.

In 1996 the "Navajo-Hopi Land Dispute Settlement Act" was passed. In return for hundreds of thousands of acres of land, the Hopi Nation agreed to grant 75-year leases to the Navajo remaining in Hopi Partitioned Land (HPL) areas. However, 26 Navajo families refused to sign leases because they claimed ownership of the land, and they continued to resist relocation. Although multiple court rulings upheld the Hopi position, no Federal action was taken, so tensions continued to mount. As of 2013, numerous bills and Congressional proposals have sought to remedy the impasse, and both the Hopi and Navajo people continue to wait for the U. S. government to provide a final resolution.

Code-Talkers

Navajo Code Talkers in Saipan during World War II

"Were it not for the Navajos, the Marines would never have taken Iwo Jima."[4] – Major Howard Connor

While numerous ethnic groups in America can be credited with contributing to the various armed conflicts the United States has participated in, Native Americans and particularly the Navajo enjoy the unique distinction of having contributed in a manner wholly reflective of their cultural heritage: the quality of their linguistic system.

Navajo "code talkers" took part in every assault the U.S. Marines conducted in the Pacific Theater from 1942 to 1945. Although the idea of devising a code using Native American language was pioneered by the Choctaw serving in the U.S. Army during World War I, and they were referred to as "Choctaw code talkers", since their involvement in World War II, code talking has been most closely associated with the Navajo.

According to U. S. military records, all early attempts to seize control of Japanese strongholds in the Pacific Theater proved calamitous because the Japanese were consistently able to break intercepted military communications. In May of 1942, the first 29 Navajo code talking recruits attended boot camp and were then sent to Camp Pendleton in California to create a code based on the Navajo language, which had never been written down and was virtually unintelligible for people who had not been exposed to it. Following the development of a dictionary, which included numerous military terms that were never part of the Navajo language, the dictionary

---

[4] *Naval History and Heritage Command website: "Navajo Code Talkers: World War II Fact Sheet."*

and all code words were then memorized. The code-talkers were ultimately able to encode, transmit, and decode a three-line English message in 20 seconds, at a time when machines required 30 minutes to complete the same process. All told, nearly 400 Navajo were trained to perform this task.

Subsequently serving in all six Marine divisions, Marine Raider battalions, and Marine parachute units at Guadalcanal, Tarawa, and Peleliu, Major Connor had six Navajo code talkers working around the clock during the first two days of the battle at Iwo Jima. They successfully sent and received over 800 messages. Other field commanders had their code talkers transmit messages by both telephone and radio in their native language, effectively broadcasting military directives the Japanese could never understand, despite the fact the Japanese were considered the best at cryptology.

Memorial to the Navajo Code Talkers in Arizona

The Navajo Code Talkers weren't initially recognized because of the continued value their language represented to national security, but on September 17, 1992, the "code talkers" of World War II were honored for their contributions to the war effort at a ceremony held at the Pentagon in Washington, D. C.

```
(srr)
 /57/
15/11-jwa                HEADQUARTERS,
                  AMPHIBIOUS FORCE, PACIFIC FLEET,
                  CAMP ELLIOTT, SAN DIEGO, CALIFORNIA

                                              March 6, 1942

      From:       The Commanding General.
      To:         The Commandant, U. S. Marine Corps.

      Subject:    Enlistment of Navaho Indians.

      Enclosures: (A) Brochure by Mr. Philip Johnston, with maps.
                  (B) Messages used in demonstration.

            1.    Mr. Philip Johnston of Los Angeles recently
      offered his services to this force to demonstrate the use of
      Indians for the transmission of messages by telephone and
      voice-radio. His offer was accepted and the demonstration
      was held for the Commanding General and his staff.

            2.    The demonstration was interesting and success-
      ful. Messages were transmitted and received almost verbatim.
      In conducting the demonstration messages were written by a
      member of the staff and handed to the Indian; he would trans-
      mit the messages in his tribal dialect and the Indian on the
      other end would write them down in English. The text of
      messages as written and received are enclosed. The Indians
      do not have many military terms in their dialect so it was
      necessary to give them a few minutes, before the demonstra-
      tion, to improvise words for dive-bombing, anti-tank gun, etc.

            3.    Mr. Johnston stated that the Navaho is the only
      tribe in the United States that has not been infested with
      German students during the past twenty years. These Germans,
      studying the various tribal dialects under the guise of art
      students, anthropologists, etc., have undoubtedly attained a
      good working knowledge of all tribal dialects except Navaho.
      For this reason the Navaho is the only tribe available offer-
      ing complete security for the type of work under consideration.
      It is noted in Mr. Johnston's article (enclosed) that the Nav-
      aho is the largest tribe but the lowest in literacy. He stat-
      ed, however, that 1,000 — if that many were needed — could
      be found with the necessary qualifications. It should also be
      noted that the Navaho tribal dialect is completely unintellig-
      ible to all other tribes and all other people, with the poss-
      ible exception of as many as 28 Americans who have made a study
      of the dialect. This dialect is thus equivalent to a secret
      code to the enemy, and admirably suited for rapid, secure com-
      munication.

                              - 1 -
```

This letter recommending the use of Navajo Code Talkers explained how the process worked.

Chapter 8: The Navajo Today

Today the Navajo Nation (*Naabeehó Bináhásdzo*) governs a territory spanning over 27,000 square miles, occupying portions of northeastern Arizona, southeastern Utah, and northwestern

New Mexico. It is the largest land area assigned primarily to a Native American jurisdiction within the United States, and it is larger than 10 of the 50 states in America.

In the Navajo language and Navajo worldview, the geographic entity known as "Naabeehó Bináhásdzo" contrasts with "Diné Bikéyah" and "Naabeehó Bikéyah" in the cultural concept of "Navajoland." These designations are not interchangeable with "Dinétah," the term used to signify the traditional sacred homeland of the Navajo people situated in the area between the mountain peaks of *Dook'o'oosłííd* (San Francisco Peaks), *Dibé Ntsaa* (Hesperus Mountain), *Sisnaajiní* (Blanca Peak), and *Tsoodził* (Mount Taylor).

Since its inception, the Navajo Nation governmental body has evolved into the largest, most sophisticated form of Native American government in North America, with the Navajo Nation Council Chambers hosting 88 council delegates representing 110 Navajo Nation chapters. Although the laws of the Navajo Nation are spelled out in the Navajo Nation Code, the United States government continues to assert "plenary power", requiring the Nation to submit all proposed laws to the U. S. Secretary of the Interior through the Bureau of Indian Affairs. The plenary power of the U. S. Congress allows them to pass laws, levy taxes, wage wars, and hold in custody those who offend federal laws. Ultimately, most conflicts and controversies between the U. S. government and the Navajo Nation are settled by negotiation and political agreements.

With a population now over 300,000, the Navajo Nation's primary objective is to sustain, maintain, and develop a viable economy for their growing numbers. While a century ago the "Rez" was regarded as little more than a desolate section of the Southwest where tourists could see "how Indians actually live", the discovery of oil in the early 1920's not only demonstrated the need for a more systematic form of government but also elevated the Navajo Nation to a wealthy nation within a nation.

To be eligible to become a member of the Navajo Nation and receive a Certificate of Indian Blood, a person must have one grandparent who was Navajo or be part of one of the four Diné clans. In 2004, the Navajo Nation Council voted down a proposal to reduce the requirement to one great-grandparent, which would have effectively doubled their registered numbers.

Today the Navajo Nation is governed by eight "Offices" (President and Vice-President, Miss Navajo Nation, Controller, Tax Commissioner, Telecommunication Regulatory Commission, Management and Budget, Washington Office, and Division of General Services) and 12 Divisions (Community Development, Department of Diné Education, Economic Development, Environmental Protection Agency, Public Safety, General Services, Health, Human Resources, Natural Resources, Social Services, Transportation, and Finance). Additionally, its Legislative Body includes Office of the Speaker, Navajo Election Administration, Auditor General, Government Development, and Nation Human Rights Commission. Its Judicial Body holds court at Kayenta.

Since the late 1960's, political factionalism has played a significant role in all major elections of the Navajo Tribal Chairmen and Councilmen. The current generation of Navajo residing on the "Rez" expects even greater factionalism as "the Navajo population increases and reservation-to-city migration results in new factional splits between reservation and off-reservation Nation members."[5] Additionally, Navajo residents living in the so-call "checkerboard area" east of the reservation proper, where many non-natives own adjoining property, have developed their own social identity. Thus, a number of sub-groups and cultures are developing within the Navajo Nation that have opposing views of what the reservation represents and what it can offer.

With mining (particularly coal and uranium) replacing the traditional Navajo economy (based on sheep and cattle herding, wool and yarn production, blanket and rug production, as well as silver and turquoise crafting), by the second half of the 20th century, the Nation had suffered considerable environmental contamination from poorly-regulated mines. As of 2005, the Navajo Nation has prohibited further uranium mining, but oil and gas leases still bring in $1.5 million per year. Additionally, the Navajo Nation's extensive mineral deposits are considered among the most valuable held by any Native American group.

Until 2004, the Navajo Nation declined to join the ranks of other Native American groups that opened gambling casinos in the United States, like the highly-successful Seminole of Florida. That year, the Nation signed its first gambling contract, a compact with New Mexico to operate a casino at *To'hajiilee* near Albuquerque. Subsequently, Navajo leaders also negotiated with Arizona officials to build casinos near Flagstaff, Lake Powell, Winslow, Sanders (*Nahata Dziil* Chapter), and Cameron (the Grand Canyon entrance). In 2004,the *Dine Development Corporation* was also formed to promote Navajo business and seek viable business opportunities in which to invest casino profits.

In early 2008, the Navajo Nation and Houston-based IPP (International Piping Products) entered into an agreement to monitor wind resources, with the potential to build a 500-megawatt wind farm about 50 miles north of Flagstaff, Arizona. Known as the "Navajo Wind Project", it will be the second commercial wind farm established in Arizona. Though approved by a tribal presidential veto in December of 2010 by the Navajo Council, disagreement between the central Navajo government and the local Navajo Cameron Chapter has led to confusion as to whether the development will materialize or not.

In the spring of 2008, the Black Mesa Water Coalition formed *Diné Binaanish Yá'át'éehgo Nooséél* (DBYN or "Navajo Green Jobs"), a coalition of organizations and individuals created to organize a "Green Jobs" initiative for the Navajo Nation. DBYN's current membership includes the Grand Canyon Trust, the Sierra Club, and New Energy Economy New Mexico, all of which seek to diversify the Navajo Nation's economy by making it more sustainable and less dependent on energy extraction and other industries that contradict traditional Navajo values regarding stewardship of the earth. Together with a number of Navajo individuals, supporting

---

[5] *Dobyns, Henry F., and Robert C. Euler.* The Navajo People. *Page 93.*

organizations, and chapters of local government, DBYN has embarked on a precedent-setting approach to addressing local concerns of economic development and environmental justice, while contributing to the well-being of the planet by reducing carbon emissions and providing more sustainable energy options in the Southwest.

In July of 2009, DBYN partnered with the Speaker of the 21st Navajo Nation Council, Lawrence T. Morgan, making the Navajo Nation the first Native America nation to adopt a "green" jobs policy. Subsequently, the "Navajo Nation Green Economy Commission" and the "Navajo Nation Green Economy Fund" were created as new entities within the tribal government to work across tribal departments to help deal with the high unemployment rate and low per capita income on the Navajo Nation by supporting "green" job opportunities.

Although famously resistant to forced education, formal education and the retention of students in all school systems is one of the Nation's primary concerns today, with disproportionately-high drop-out rates among high school students still remaining a major problem. Over 150 public, private, and Bureau of Indian Affairs schools serve Navajo students from kindergarten through high school, with most schools receiving funding from the Navajo Nation under the Johnson O'Malley program. That program was designed to address the unique cultural needs of Native American students. Post-secondary education and vocational training are also available on and off reservation. The Nation also operates Diné College, a two-year community college with its main campus in Tsaile (in Apache County), as well as seven other campuses on the reservation. Founded in 1968, Diné College was the first tribal college in the U. S., and it currently has a student body over 1,800.

The Nation also runs a local Head Start Program that provides comprehensive education, health, nutrition, and parent involvement services to low-income Native American children and their families. It is the only educational program operated by the Navajo Nation government. Since drop-out rates are disproportionally high on the Navajo "Rez," the Nation has adopted programs such as the "Literacy is Empowering Project" to help combat academic problems, a non-profit project that promotes literacy and pre-reading skills for Native American children to increase their understanding of standard academic language.

Currently, several types of cancer occur on the Navajo Reservation at markedly higher rates than the nation at large, particularly reproductive-organ cancers in teenage Navajo girls at an average of 17 times higher than the national average. Additionally, diabetes mellitus is a major health concern, occurring about 4 times more often than the national average. Furthermore, 1 in 2500 Navajo children inherits Severe Combined Immunodeficiency (SCID), a genetic disorder that results in children having virtually no natural defense system whatsoever.

Today the Navajo Nation and its people represent not just a chapter from America's colonial history but a tribute to its multicultural present, and an insight into its future. Proving one of the most adaptive indigenous groups ever to settle North America, their success in establishing a homeland, developing a viable and adaptive economy, and utilizing their natural resources to benefit and empower their people serves as a model of perseverance and resolve. From their ranchers to their warriors, athletes to their artisans, the Navajo people have advanced their own interests and contributed to the cultural fabric of the United States of America.

Bibliography

Adair, David F. *Navajo and Pueblo Silversmiths*. Norman, OK: University of Oklahoma Press, 1945.

Beard, Charles A., and Mary R. Beard. The Beards' New Basic History of the United States. *New York: Doubleday & Company, Inc., 1960.*

Dobyns, Henry F., and Robert C. Euler. The Navajo People. *Phoenix, AZ: Indian Tribal Series, 1972.*

Dyk, Walter. A Navaho Autobiography. *New York: Viking Fund Publication No. 8, 1947.*

Erdoes, Richard, and Alfonso Ortiz. American Indian Myths and Legends. *New York: Pantheon Books, 1984.*

Gilpin, Laura. The Enduring Navajo. *Austin, TX: University of Texas Press, 1968.*

Kluckhohn, Clyde. Navaho Witchcraft. *Boston, MA: Beacon Press, 1944.*

Leagle.com website: "Healing vs. Jones": http://www.leagle.com/xmlResult.aspx?xmldoc=1959385174FSupp211_1363.xml&docbase=CSLWAR1-1950-1985. Accessed 03.20.2013.

Maxwell, J. A. The First Americans: Their Customs, Art, History, and How They Lived. *New York: Readers Digest Press, 1978.*

Moss, Joyce, and George Wilson. Peoples of the World: North Americans. *Detroit, MI: Gale Research, Inc., 1991.*

Navajo-Hopi Long Land Dispute: Accessed via http://www.kstrom.net/isk/maps/az/navhopi.html. 03.20.2013.

Navajo Nation Government website: http://www.navajo-nsn.gov/. Accessed 03.19.2013.

Navajo People—the Diné website: http://navajopeople.org/. Accessed 03.19.2013.

NavajoTimes.com website: http://navajotimes.com/. Accessed 03.21.2013.

Naval History and Heritage Command website: "Navajo Code Talkers: World War II Fact

Sheet." Accessed via *http://www.history.navy.mil/faqs/faq61-2.htm 03.25.2013.*

Neusius, Sarah, W., and G. Timothy Gross. Seeking Our Past: An Introduction to North American Archaeology. *Oxford: Oxford University Press, 2007.*

Sides, Hampton. Blood and Thunder. *New York: Doubleday, 2006.*

Wilson, James. The Earth Shall Weep. *New York: Atlantic Monthly Press, 1998.*

Printed in Great Britain
by Amazon.co.uk, Ltd.,
Marston Gate.